NATURE IN CLOSE-UP

THE GARDEN SPIDER

JAN ETHELBERG

ADAM & CHARLES BLACK   LONDON

Published by A & C Black Ltd, 35 Bedford Row, London WC1
First published in this edition 1976. Originally published by Borgens Forlag A/S, Copenhagen, as *Korsedderkoppen*
© 1973 Jan Ethelberg and 1976 A & C Black Ltd (English edition)
ISBN 0 7136 1635 0
Printed in Great Britain by Colour Craftsmen

Spiders' webs

Spiders make webs in many different shapes: some webs are tightly-woven and look like hammocks; others form a loose open network between the branches of trees.

Spiders build webs to catch insects. Some spiders do not build webs, because they chase and catch their prey on the ground. There is even one kind of spider which spends its whole life under water.

The garden spider builds a large web with threads stretching out from the centre, like the spokes in a wheel, and fine threads going round from spoke to spoke in a spiral.

Where the garden spider lives

The garden spider lives in woods, parks or gardens—wherever it can build its web on leaves or twigs.

It likes to build its web vertically, sometimes by forest paths like the one in the photograph. The web catches flying insects. The spider often waits in the centre of its web, head downwards. Sometimes it hides among the leaves, but it is always attached to its web by a thread and can feel the slightest movement in the web.

What the garden spider looks like

It has white markings in the shape of a cross on its back. This is why it is sometimes called the cross spider. It has eight legs and a brown hairy body.

The two upper jaws have poison fangs for paralysing the prey. The lower jaws look like an extra pair of legs. They are used for holding the prey while eating.

The head is seen between the legs. It has eight eyes. On the underside of the head are four jaws.

Underneath the hind part of the body are six *spinnerets* and an anus. Nearer the front are the sexual parts and two slits which lead to the 'lungs'.

The spinnerets make the thread for building a web. You can see fine threads coming out of the back end of the spider.

How the spider builds its web

The garden spider starts building very early in the morning, sometimes before sunrise.

It lets a few threads flutter in the wind. When one of these meets a leaf or twig, it sticks. The spider tightens this thread and strengthens it with more threads.

Now it makes the frame of the web. It lowers itself from one end of the strong thread on to another leaf or twig and fastens the thread there. Then it raises itself, with thread still coming out behind, and joins the thread to other supports. It spins more thread and secures it to other leaves, making a five-sided frame. Follow the diagrams to see how the spider builds from here.

It is the female garden spider which builds the big web which you can find. The male builds a smaller, shabbier web.

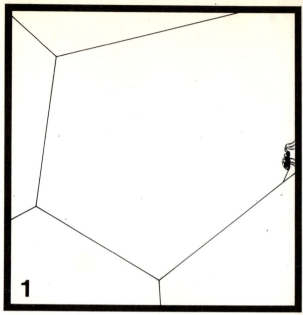

The spider has nearly finished the frame.

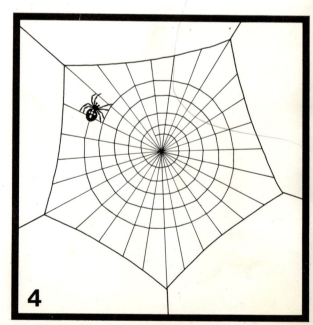

The spider then spins a wide spiral from the centre towards the frame. It uses dry thread.

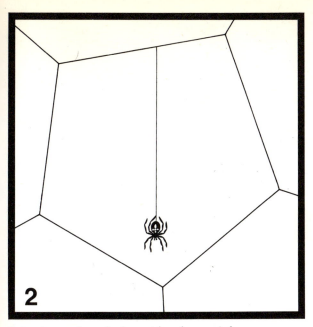

2

Spinning a thread, the spider drops right across the finished frame. This is the first spoke.

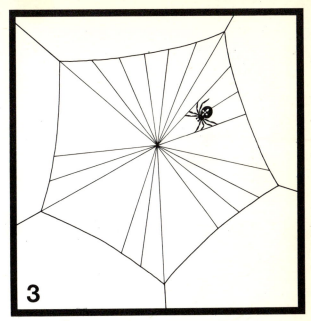

3

It spins threads all the way round. All the spokes are equally tight.

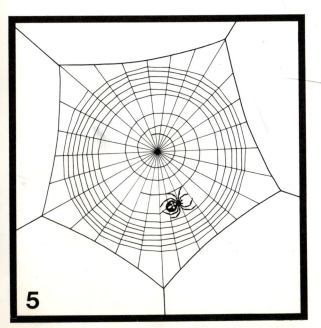

5

Now it spins a spiral of thread in the opposite direction. This is the spiral for catching insects. It is sticky with glue.

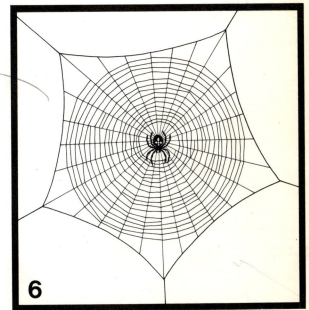

6

On its way back to the centre, the spider removes the first, wide spiral which was only for walking on.

The garden spider waits, head down, in the centre of its web. When insects fly into the web they are caught by the sticky threads. The spider is not caught by its own web because it has an oily liquid on its feet which counteracts the glue.

Throughout the day, wind, rain, fallen leaves and captured insects damage the web. In the evening the spider removes all but the frame of the old web. It spends the night among the leaves and builds a new web next morning.

The spider fixes the sticky catching thread onto one spoke and then pulls it round from spoke to spoke.

It pulls the thread out with one leg . . .

. . . then with the other. This keeps the thread neither too tight nor too slack.

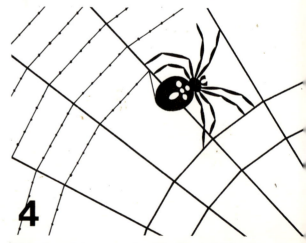

This thread is covered with glue which contracts to form a row of sticky drops.

The spider works without stopping when building its web. It only takes about an hour.

This is part of a finished web. The white spots on the spokes are the remains of the first spiral.

The garden spider's food

The garden spider eats insects which blunder into its web. Large strong insects can tear their way free, but flies, mosquitoes, lace-wing flies and crane flies get hopelessly caught up in the sticky threads.

If a wasp gets entangled in the web, the spider hurries to cut the threads and help it escape. The spider fears the wasp's sting. The spider also frees leaves in the same way, to prevent them ruining the web.

In late summer the females build their webs closer to the ground. There are fewer flying insects to catch, but plenty of grasshoppers which may jump into the web.

The spider catches a fly

1. A large fly has flown into the web. It struggles to escape but only gets more and more caught up.

2. At the first movement of the web the spider rushes to its prey.

3. The spider paralyses the fly with its poison fangs. The poison stops the fly struggling but does not kill it.

4. The spider wraps up the fly in a mass of silk threads. It is not yet ready to eat the fly. The fly is not dead, so it will keep fresh for some time.

A meal

5. The spider drags the fly to the centre of the web to eat it. The spider has no teeth to chew its food, only a small hole leading to its stomach. From its stomach it pours out a juice over its prey. This juice dissolves the fly into a kind of soup which the spider can absorb.

6. A meal lasts nearly all day. All that is left at the end is a small black lump which is pushed out of the web.

7. Crane flies are easily caught in the web because of their long legs.

8. This garden spider has caught a lace-wing fly.

This leaf has blown into the web.

The spider quickly cuts the threads around the leaf.

The leaf is soon free and falls to the ground. The spider will have to repair the damage to its web.

The spider sheds its skin

The garden spider grows quite a lot during its life, but its skin does not grow, so it has to change its skin several times.

The spider hides quietly among some leaves for a few days. Early one morning its skin splits and it wriggles free. A new skin has grown underneath. The old skin is pushed away, as you can see in the photograph opposite.

The spider stays in hiding for a few more days while its new skin grows strong and supple.

Courtship

1. At the end of his second summer the male spider sheds his skin for the last time. He is now ready to court a female. He spins a small silk cushion on a leaf and drops some sperm from the hind part of his body onto this cushion. Then he turns round and sucks the sperm into small reservoirs in his lower jaw. When the male finds a female on her web he sits warily on some leaves nearby.

The male is much smaller and narrower than the female and his lower jaw is swollen. The female has grown fat with eggs.

2. The male spins a few threads which blow in the wind until they stick to the female's web. He tightens these threads and begins to pluck them with his front legs. This makes her web vibrate.

3. The female notices the vibrations at once, but she is busy eating. The male approaches cautiously. He keeps a safety thread attached to the leaves so that he can escape quickly.

4. Now she sees him and leaves her prey. He dances in front of her. He does not want to be mistaken for a fly. If she thought he was a fly, she would attack and poison him.

5. He rises on his eight legs, broadens, wriggles from side to side and dances for her. Sometimes she frightens him off, but he soon returns to dance.

6. Suddenly she pulls her legs in close to her body. He rushes up and presses his lower jaw on to the hind part of her body, gives her his sperm and leaps away again.

7. He does this a second time.

8. She chases him away. He scuttles out of her reach, lowers himself on his safety thread and hides among the leaves.

9. The female crawls back to the trapped bee she was eating before. The male dies a few days after courtship.

The eggs are laid

1. Now it is autumn. The female still builds a web, but not every day. The mornings are damp and cool and the heavy dew damages her web. The web is no longer sticky and barely hangs together.

2. The female, who is fat and round with eggs, leaves her web. She crawls away and finds an old fence post where she hides in a crack.

3. If you find a fat female spider before she has laid her eggs you can catch her carefully and take her home to watch her lay her eggs. Give her some bark to lay the eggs on.

4. Late one evening she spins a silk cushion on the inside of the bark. She lays her eggs on this cushion. At the same time, lots of yellow thread comes out of her spinnerets until the eggs are completely covered by a yellow cocoon of threads. She lays more than 200 eggs, until her body is thin again.

5. You can see the yellow cocoon on the bark near the bottom of the fence post on the right.

6. The female camouflages the cocoon with dust and bits of bark. She dies soon after she has finished.

7. The eggs remain hidden all through the winter.

8. The eggs look like this inside their cocoon.

The young spiders hatch out

1. Each egg is one millimetre long. It is pale gold in colour throughout winter. You can see the threads of the cocoon.

2. In spring the egg turns a darker colour. The young spider in the egg begins to develop.

3. You can just see a faint suggestion of legs inside the egg.

4. One morning in May the young spider struggles out of its shell.

5. All the spiders in the cocoon hatch at the same time. If you look very closely, you will see that this is a mass of tiny, pale yellow spiders crawling over each other.

6. The young spiders gradually turn a deeper colour, and their legs look almost black. They stay in hiding for about a week and shed their skin for the first time.

7. When the little spiders come out of hiding, they are bright gold with a black triangle on the hind part of the body.

8. They spin long, almost invisible threads. The wind lifts them by these threads and blows them over fields, ditches and bushes.

Opposite page: A group of young spiders has settled on a privet hedge and started to build their first webs. Each web is a small version of the adult's web and catches only small insects. It is easily damaged. Young spiders often have to rebuild their web several times in a day.

A young spider eats its first meal.

The young spiders grow quickly. In a few months they are about four millimetres long and have a distinct little cross on their back. They hibernate during the winter among leaves or under bark until the following year, when they are fully grown.

Some facts about the garden spider

The garden spider (like all spiders) belongs to a group of animals called Arachnids. Harvestmen and mites are also Arachnids. The Latin name for the garden spider is *Epeira diademata*.

The Arachnids are divided into groups, and the garden spider belongs to a group called *Orb weavers*, which all make circular webs. There are several hundred different kinds of spider in Britain, each with its own special type of web.

The garden spider lives for about two years and can grow as large as 14 millimetres long, excluding the legs. It is found in Europe and in Asia.

The adult's web can be as much as 50 cm in diameter. The spider's poison is not dangerous to humans. Most spiders usually try to hide if you disturb them.

Some experiments to try

Catch a spider in a box and bring it home. Adult spiders are easier to catch than young ones because they move more slowly. Put it on a bush near the house, or on some leafy twigs in the house, and it may build a web. See if you can catch some live flies to feed it with, and watch how it deals with its prey. Try throwing a small leaf into the web. What happens?

Try copying the way the spider makes drops of glue along its catching thread: mix a little gloy with water so that it is fairly runny; hold a hair from your head between your fingers and spread it with the thinned gloy. Pull it tight. What happens?

Try touching the sticky threads of the spider's web with dry fingers. What happens? Now touch them with oily fingers. What happens? When your fingers are dry, they are like a fly's feet. When they are oily, they are like a spider's feet.